A Note to Readers

I was fifteen years old when I participated in my first Paralympic Games. It took my breath away. There I was, competing on the world stage. Being recognized as an elite athlete. Being honored for excellence in sport. It changed my life.

People with disabilities are so often treated as second-class citizens. Wheelchair users are left behind because they can't get up the stairs. Individuals with visual impairments can't safely navigate challenging terrain. And amputees don't look like everyone else. When you have a disability, others often make decisions for you, believing they know what you can and cannot do. Those decisions have a lifelong impact, often limiting our achievements and limiting our success.

The Paralympic Games changed all that by creating a forum where competitors, regardless of their disability, are treated as first-class citizens and recognized for their athleticism, their bravery, and their determination.

The Paralympic Games are a true celebration of what is best about athletic competition—bringing together individuals from all over the world to celebrate inclusion, equality, courage, fairness, friendship, loyalty, patriotism, and sport. World Records are broken, medals are given, and barriers are removed.

Spectators, in the stadium or at home, are treated to competition between some of the world's most elite athletes while learning that people with disabilities aren't so different after all.

Fifteen years have passed since my first Paralympic Games in Athens, Greece, in 2004. In that time, recognition of the Paralympic Games, and individual Paralympic athletes, has grown exponentially. The Games are now the third-largest sporting event in the world. The publication of *What Are the Paralympic Games?* represents one more giant step forward in acknowledging and accepting people with disabilities as equal citizens in our global society.

Tatyana McFadden
Paralympic Gold Medal Racer

What Are the Paralympic Games?

by Gail Herman

illustrated by Andrew Thomson

Penguin Workshop

To Jane, oh-so-insightful editor—GH

To Rhia and baby Thomson—AT

PENGUIN WORKSHOP
An Imprint of Penguin Random House LLC, New York

Library of Congress Control Number: 2019034728

ISBN 9781524792626 (paperback)   10 9 8 7 6 5 4 3 2 1
ISBN 9781524792633 (library binding)   10 9 8 7 6 5 4 3 2 1

Contents

What Are the Paralympic Games?

It is a humid September evening in 2016. At the Maracanã Stadium in Rio de Janeiro, Brazil, more than seventy thousand spectators fill the seats for the opening ceremony of the fifteenth Summer Paralympics. Seventeen days earlier, the closing ceremony for the Olympics took place here, too.

The Olympics and the Paralympics both feature summer and winter games. Both are held every four years. And thousands of athletes from around the world gather to compete in both sets of games.

There's one real difference: At the Paralympics, the athletes have a range of disabilities—any conditions that somehow limit movement or activity. Some swim without arms, race without legs, or run without sight.

The opening ceremony begins with a parade of athletes entering the stadium. Teams arrive from over 160 countries, each led by a flag-bearer. Some athletes are in wheelchairs, some have guides, and some wear prosthetics—artificial limbs. Speeches are given, and music is played. Performers take the stage.

Then an announcement is made. "Ladies and gentlemen, the Paralympic flame!" After a relay across Brazil, the torch arrives.

Marcia Malsar receives the torch just as it starts to rain. Water drenches Malsar, who must use a cane to cross the stage. She raises the flame above her head. Suddenly, she slips and falls. The torch drops to the ground.

Immediately, Malsar gets to her feet. Someone holds out the torch. She takes it, smiling. The crowd roars with approval. So do the other athletes. They understand that when you fall, you just get up again.

Now Marcia delivers the torch to the next in line. The cauldron is lit. Fireworks explode.

Let the Games begin!

CHAPTER 1
The Idea Forms

The Paralympics began with one doctor's vision: He believed that paraplegics—people who can't move their legs or lower body—could lead full, useful lives. Many other doctors at the time didn't think they could improve the health or well-being of people in wheelchairs, so they didn't even try.

During the years after World War II, Dr. Ludwig Guttmann saw hospitals filled with wounded soldiers, many with spinal cord injuries. At the Stoke Mandeville Hospital in England, Guttmann created workshops and classes designed to get the patients moving.

One afternoon Guttmann jumped in a wheelchair to join patients hitting a puck with canes. *Why not have team sports, too?* he thought. Another day, he brought in bows and arrows for archery.

Dr. Ludwig Guttmann

Doctors in other hospitals soon adopted Guttmann's program. And that gave Guttmann another idea: to host a sports competition between hospitals.

In 1948, the first Stoke Mandeville Games for the Paralyzed took place. He chose the date with care: July 29. It was the same day as the opening ceremony of the Olympics in nearby London.

Already, Guttmann had a plan to have an Olympics for those with disabilities.

Of course, no one would confuse the first Stoke Mandeville Games with the Olympics. There was just one sport, archery, and only two teams. Fourteen men and two women competed.

But the Games were such a success that Guttmann decided to hold them every year. Each year, more events were added. Soon there were wheelchair races on the track and swimmers in the pool.

In 1952, the Games welcomed a team from another country, the Netherlands. By the time the United States sent a group in 1955, there were seventeen other countries competing. The International Olympic Committee took notice. The next year, it gave Guttmann's Stoke Mandeville Games an award for outstanding Olympic ideals.

Years passed and the Games added a flag,

Olympic rings logo

a parade of athletes, and an opening day relay. Instead of a torch, "runners" who traveled by car and wheelchair carried a scroll stating the Paralympic mission: "To unite paralyzed men and women from all parts of the world . . . [to] give hope and inspiration to thousands of paralyzed people." In the very first relay, in 1958, Dick Thompson brought the scroll home to Stoke Mandeville.

At the Games, Thompson was already a star. At the age of seventeen, he had broken his back in a climbing accident. He wound up paralyzed from the chest down. One year later, in 1950, he won the javelin event, a throwing contest.

The javelin is a long spear, and in the nondisabled sport, a thrower gets a running start. But wheelchair throwers are seated—and remain at a standstill—using only shoulder strength, not momentum, to hurl the javelin.

Thompson's first winning throw was forty-six feet, one inch.

At one event, Thompson even competed against two nondisabled men: the British javelin and shot put champions. Guttmann sat them down in wheelchairs. Thompson beat them both.

Then came 1960. The Olympics had just been held in Rome. And Thompson, along with wheelchair teams from more than twenty countries, was headed there, too. Guttmann's dream was coming true. After all, what better way was there for the Paralympics to be like the Olympics than for it to share a host city?

CHAPTER 2
The Early Years

The 1960 Games are considered the first international Paralympics, and Margaret Maughan was thrilled to be part of them.

Margaret Maughan

Just a year and a half earlier, Maughan had been in a car accident. She would never walk again. At Stoke Mandeville, she took up archery. She was a natural. For Maughan, making Great Britain's team was the easy part. However, getting on an airplane meant being raised to the airplane door by a forklift.

In Rome, teams had to stay in buildings without elevators. Luckily, the Italian army was called in to help. They were stationed on landings to carry people up and down the steep stairs.

No TV cameras focused on these four hundred or so para-athletes. There were no cheering crowds at Margaret Maughan's archery event. Maughan wasn't even sure there were officials keeping score.

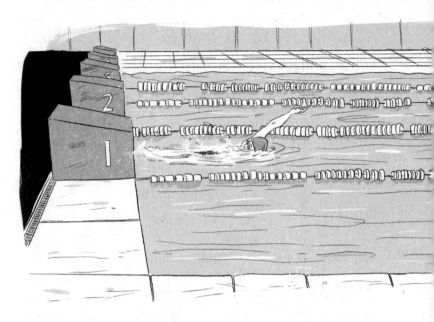

She had no idea how she'd done until she was on a bus and someone told her she was wanted at the awards ceremony. She had won a gold medal.

Like most everyone else, Maughan competed in more than one sport. Wheelchair racers played basketball. Fencers threw the shot put. With little funding, only a small group of British athletes was able to go. They had to cover all different events. Maughan won a gold in swimming for a backstroke event where she was the only

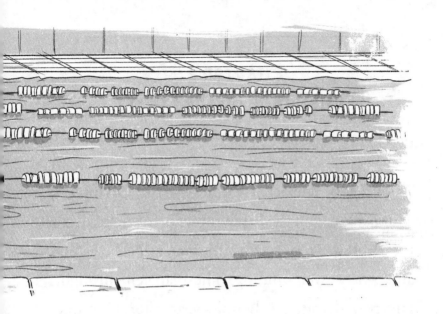

contestant in the pool.

In 1964, the next Olympic year, Paralympic teams traveled to Tokyo. They competed right after the Olympians. Once again, the two events shared one host city. They were tied together, part of Guttmann's Paralympic plan.

But the connection wouldn't last.

CHAPTER 3
Challenge on the Court

In 1968, Mexico City hosted the Olympics. There was talk of the Paralympics being held there, too. But there was concern over athletes' safety and worry over funding. The plan fell through. For two decades, Olympic year after Olympic year, other host cities couldn't—or wouldn't—take on the Paralympics.

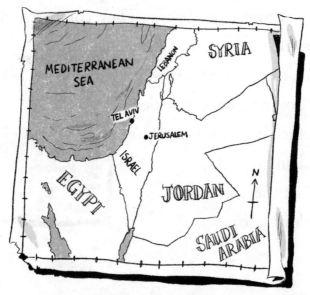

Fortunately, in '68, the city of Tel Aviv, Israel, stepped in to host. Excitement gripped the new country, which was just twenty years old.

The biggest draw there was the gold medal game in wheelchair basketball, Israel versus the United States.

Every seat in the sports center was taken. People packed the street outside, and even the players' families had trouble getting in. Israel won, 47–37, led by team captain Baruch Hagai. At twenty-four, he was the star of the squad.

Four years later, Hagai and the Israeli team flew to Heidelberg, Germany, for the next Paralympics. And once again, they faced the United States in the title game.

Like all wheelchair basketball games, it was played on a regulation court, with baskets at the usual height. Players pushed their chairs while dribbling or held the ball in their lap for two pushes before they shot, passed, or dribbled again.

Early in the second half, Hagai scored sixteen points in a row. Somehow, the United States

stayed in the game. With under a minute left of play, Israel was up by five. The US team had to step up—big-time.

They made the next basket. But there were only thirteen seconds left. American Ed Owen had the ball. He took a long shot, making the two-pointer. The score: 58–57. The United States still had a chance.

An Israeli player was making the inbound pass. Quickly, Owen wheeled down the court,

intercepting the ball. A second later, he aimed for the hoop. Hagai rushed to Owen. He stretched up as high as he could, straining against the wheelchair footrest, to block the play. He couldn't.

Swish! The United States won, 59–58.

In 1976, the United States beat Israel again for the gold. But before those Summer Games could begin, the very first Winter Games took place.

The Paralympic movement was growing.

CHAPTER 4
Growth and Change

The Winter Paralympics started small in Ornskoldsvik, Sweden. There were fewer than two hundred athletes and only two sports: downhill and cross-country skiing. But the Games brought big changes.

Instead of limiting competitors to those with spinal cord injuries—like at the Summer Games—these Paralympics included other disability groups. There were athletes with missing limbs and those with visual impairments.

That first Winter Paralympics paved the way for changes in the Summer Games, too. In '76, athletes with missing limbs and people with vision loss competed in Toronto, Canada.

Almost from the beginning, competitors had been placed in groups—sports classifications—based on their spinal cord disability. The idea was to have a level playing field for all the athletes. Now, to cover the different disability groups, more classes were added.

More classes meant more competitors. And more competitors meant more interest. Reporters had covered the Games before. But in 1976, for the first time, events were shown on regional TV stations every day.

The Paralympics were getting attention. Still, one British athlete discovered there was a long way to go.

At twenty-six years old, Mike Kenny had a spinal cord injury so severe, he could only blink his eyes. Little by little, he regained strength in his upper body. Mike had always loved swimming,

Mike Kenny

and even though it was scary, he decided to try it again. At his first Games in Toronto, Kenny broke para-athlete world records in three different events. His wife contacted British newspapers. This had to be big news, she thought. But not one paper ran the story.

After three more Paralympics, Kenny retired with a total of eighteen medals. He'd be Great Britain's most decorated para-athlete for decades to come. But hardly anyone knew his name.

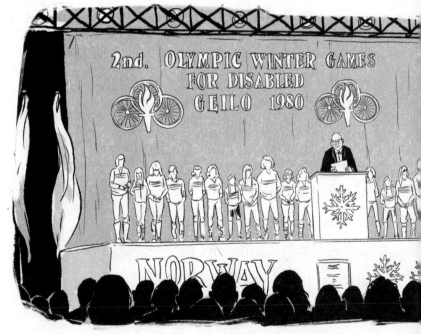

In the meantime, the second Winter Paralympics, held in Geilo, Norway, in 1980, grew bigger and better, with events for athletes with spinal cord injuries, too. Sadly, Ludwig Guttmann was too ill to travel to the Winter Games in 1980. He died a month later. When the Summer Games opened in June, a moment of silence honored the visionary doctor.

And the most decorated athlete in Paralympic history was about to dive into the pool.

Sports Classifications

At first, classifications were medical groups, so a person with a spinal cord injury competed against other people with spinal cord injuries. The system evolved over time so that now athletes with different disabilities are grouped together. It all depends on the physical requirements of each event and how a disability affects competing. Sometimes, when players have different impairment levels, a mathematical formula computes a fair score or race time.

SPORT	AMPUTEE	BLIND/ VISUALLY IMPAIRED	SPINAL CORD INJURY	TRAUMATIC BRAIN INJURY / CEREBRAL PALSY / STROKE	INTELLECTUAL IMPAIRMENT
ARCHERY	☆		☆	☆	
BOCCIA				☆	
CANOE	☆		☆	☆	
CYCLING	☆	☆	☆	☆	
EQUESTRIAN	☆	☆	☆	☆	
GOALBALL		☆			
JUDO		☆			
POWERLIFTING	☆		☆	☆	
ROWING	☆	☆	☆	☆	
SAILING	☆	☆	☆	☆	
SHOOTING	☆		☆	☆	

Paralympic sports classification grid

CHAPTER 5
Legend in the Pool

In 1980, the Dutch city of Arnhem hosted the Summer Paralympic Games—and sixteen-year-old Trischa Zorn was the youngest member of the US team. Born with limited vision, Zorn could barely make out objects and people, even when standing close to them. In the water, that didn't matter.

Growing up in Orange County, California, Zorn struggled in school. There were no large-print books or computers. She had little support. Swimming took her away from all that.

In the Pool

In the water, swimmers who are blind are helped by "tappers." Every swimmer has one tapper standing at each end of the pool. These assistants hold a tapping device—usually a pole with a ball at the end—and alert swimmers when they're about to reach a wall by tapping them on the head or the back. Swimmers train to make sure they stay in their lanes, learning to feel for the rope as they go.

In the Netherlands, Zorn won seven gold medals, for the 100m freestyle and for the 100m backstroke, among others. At the next Games, she won five, and at the one after that, an unbelievable twelve. For twenty-four years and seven Paralympics, she stepped up to the winners' podium again and again. Ultimately, she earned fifty-five medals, the most of any Paralympian. But her most memorable one came last.

It was 2004 and Zorn was forty years old. Just a few months earlier, her mother had passed away. She'd cheered on Zorn at every Paralympics before this one. Heartbroken, Zorn stopped training for a time. She needed time to grieve. Still, she came to the Games ready to do her best.

In her first race, Zorn came in seventh. Then came her last chance, the 100m backstroke. This time, she won a medal. It wasn't gold, and it wasn't silver. But this bronze she counted as her favorite medal ever.

"It was a tribute to my mom," she explained.

While Zorn swam her way through the '80s (and '90s and beyond), the Paralympics kept growing. And the focus of the Games shifted. They weren't just a way to help people recover from injury. Now athletes had coaches. They trained longer and harder. The performance level rose. The Games became more about competition.

They were turning into events for super-serious athletes, just like the Olympics. And in 1988, the connection was about to get stronger.

On the Court

Goalball: Three-player teams face each other across a rectangular court, with nets stretching behind each team. To score, players throw a heavy, hard rubber ball—filled with bells—into the other team's net while their opponents try to block it.

Five-a-side soccer: Players kick a noise-making soccer ball on a court surrounded by special boards that echo when players snap their fingers. Coaches stand on the sidelines, shouting directions to the offense, while the sighted or partially sighted goalie instructs the defense. Athletes call out "Voy"—Spanish for "I am here"—when they're on defense, to alert the attacking players.

CHAPTER 6
Paralympic Breakthroughs

In the summer of 1988, for the first time in more than twenty years, the Paralympics were going to be held in the same city as the Olympics: Seoul, South Korea. In fact, the Paralympics and Olympics would share the same host city from there on out for both Summer and Winter Games.

Opening ceremony of the 1988 Olympics in Seoul, South Korea

There were other changes, too. Officials made sure to keep careful records. The Soviet Union—made up of Russia and other, smaller countries—sent its first team. All over the world, people with disabilities were being recognized.

In 1992, the Summer Games in Barcelona, Spain, proved to be another high point. One athlete lit the cauldron for both the Olympics and Paralympics. *And* he was a Paralympian. At both opening ceremonies, the para-archer Antonio Rebello sent a flaming arrow shooting across the night sky. It was caught on TV—the Games were televised every day.

The Americans with Disabilities Act

The Americans with Disabilities Act became law in 1990. Modeled after the Civil Rights Act of 1964, it guarantees people with impairments equal treatment and opportunities—in education, housing, transportation, and employment—so they can fully take part in all areas of life. Hotels, restaurants, schools, and buses were now required to have a way for all people to use them. For

instance, sometimes that meant adding wheelchair ramps and elevators. And those with disabilities could not be turned away when applying for a job or getting a home.

The Winter Games were big news, too. The French president opened the Albertville Paralympics in 1992. A record twenty-four countries participated.

German downhill skier Reinhild Möller was the star of the Games, winning four gold medals in the standing category.

Reinhild Möller

Möller didn't have long to wait for the next Winter Paralympics. They were going to take place in 1994. It was part of the new schedule, with Summer and Winter Games alternating every two years just like the Olympics. And, in Lillehammer, Norway, Möller would have another stellar showing.

At three years old, Reinhild Möller lost a leg in an accident on her family's farm. She grew up using a prosthetic leg, playing all sorts of sports with able-bodied classmates. But Möller didn't stop there. She competed in Winter *and* Summer Paralympics. She never stopped training, and she didn't earn a cent for her efforts.

Companies paid nondisabled athletes money to advertise their products, use their gear, or wear their clothes while they trained and competed. Möller wanted that, too.

After her big wins, Möller's sponsor, a German building company, offered her a million-dollar contract. No athlete with a disability had ever earned that kind of money. It was a landmark moment. It showed that the public cared about Paralympians and saw them as role models.

Skiing with Physical Disabilities

There are three categories in each skiing event: one for competitors with a visual impairment and two more categories—standing and sitting—for those with another kind of physical disability.

Some standing skiers race on one ski; others use prosthetics and two skis. Athletes with an arm impairment can use one pole or even none. Sit-skiers use a specially molded seat placed on one wide ski for downhill events and two narrow skis for cross-country.

CHAPTER 7
Wheels on the Track

Two years later, in 1996, Atlanta, Georgia, hosted the Summer Games. Australian wheelchair racer Louise Sauvage competed in the 400m, 800m, 1500m, and 5000m races. She took gold in every event. Canada's Chantal Petitclerc won

Louise Sauvage and Chantal Petitclerc at the
1996 Summer Paralympic Games

gold in all her events, too—except when she raced against Sauvage.

But Petitclerc knew the two would meet again. The next Games were in Sydney, Australia. Sauvage was huge there, the hometown favorite. Still, Petitclerc now held the world record for their 800m contest.

As soon as the starting gun sounded, Petitclerc exploded from the line. Seconds later, the racers passed the first curve. In longer races, athletes start out in individual lanes, then "cut in" after a curve, jockeying for a top spot along the inside track. It's always a scramble, but Petitclerc took the lead. Sauvage was a very close third.

The racers barreled down the straightaway. They took the second curve, their chairs swerving around the bend. In the back of the pack, two racers lost control. They crashed, taking a third racer out, too.

Then in the final lap, another racer pulled ahead of both Petitclerc and Sauvage.

Heads down, Petitclerc and Sauvage pushed even harder. They picked up speed, passing the front-runner on the outside.

Once again, Petitclerc was in first. Sauvage inched closer, her front wheel right by Petitclerc's rear one. The crowd urged Sauvage on. But she couldn't gain ground. Petitclerc crossed the finish line for the gold.

Wheelchair Racing

In early wheelchair racing, chairs weighed fifty pounds or more. Today's racing chairs, long and low to the ground, can weigh as little as fifteen pounds, with one small wheel in front and two larger ones in back. They go faster than twenty miles per hour on a level track.

Racers sit with their legs tucked under the seat, holding their head down, and their shoulders in position to push the wheels in a strong downward motion. The movement requires great upper body strength. Athletes train on long road "pushes" to build up endurance and shorter, more intense rides around the track to increase speed.

Sauvage retired after the 2000 Games, and Petitclerc went on to sweep the competition in the next two Paralympics. Altogether, she won fourteen gold medals. And she never lost her fighting spirit. But when she received the Athlete of the Year Award from Athletics Canada in 2004, she refused the honor.

Why?

The organization had named another winner as well, an Olympic sprinter. But the nondisabled runner had lost her race, falling flat on her face. Petitclerc felt the award should have been hers alone. To her, sharing it with an athlete who had messed up a race showed that para-athletes weren't taken seriously enough. Their efforts didn't mean as much.

On behalf of all disabled athletes, Petitclerc felt it wasn't right to share the award.

CHAPTER 8
A Victory, a Scandal, and a Record

Paralympians who are blind always share their medals. That is because they compete with a guide. When one wins, so does the other.

Take Henry Wanyoike, for instance. As he was growing up in Kenya, his eyesight was perfectly fine. And he'd always been a runner,

Henry Wanyoike

hoping to make the Olympic team. But when he was only twenty-one years old, Wanyoike had a stroke—a sudden blockage in the brain's blood supply. Doctors thought he had recovered.

Then, two months later, he woke up and couldn't see. But he learned that he could still run. All he needed was a guide.

Guides are connected to their runner by a band around their wrists and match their stride and speed to their partner's gait, keeping in sync. This new way of running took time to master. But one year later, Wanyoike made it to the 2000 Games in Sydney. His 5000m race started well. Then his guide slowed down. Every step became a struggle for the guide. He was sick. The race was wearing him down.

By sheer force of will, Wanyoike pulled him along, down the straightaway, over the finish line—right into first place!

Guides and runners need a special bond. The runner must trust the guide completely, since they call out information about the track, the other runners, and how far they have to go. Sometimes the guide is a professional runner, too, and sometimes the runner chooses a partner about the same height to make tandem running easier.

But Wanyoike decided a strong bond was most important.

After the 2000 Games, Wanyoike asked his childhood friend Joseph Kibunja to be his guide. They trained hard together, sharing a true trust. At the next Paralympics, they smashed two world records.

Back in Kenya, Wanyoike helped change the country's constitution so that all types of people—including those with disabilities—would be represented in the government. "I lost my sight, but I never lost my vision," he's always said.

Wanyoike's triumph at Sydney had been a struggle. Not so for the Spanish men's basketball team at that same Paralympics. They sailed to victory. But everything wasn't what it seemed.

Spanish men's basketball team, 2000 Paralympic Games in Sydney

The team played in the classification for athletes with intellectual disabilities. But only two players had an impairment. The others were semipro players. They used fake information to pass the Paralympic review. Why was the team being so dishonest? To boost Spain's medal count.

They might have gotten away with it, except one player was an undercover journalist. He'd planned all along to tell the truth. And he did, publishing a front-page story in a magazine.

The news rocked the Paralympics. The case went to court. Policies and tests had to be changed. The intellectual disability program shut down for twelve years while organizers figured out a fair system. That meant that many athletes at the peak of their performance missed out on the Paralympics altogether. It hardly seems fair.

But of course the Games went on.

The Special Olympics

Special Olympics

Founded in 1968, the Special Olympics supports people with intellectual disabilities. There are year-round sports programs, open to all regardless of sports ability. All athletes are recognized for their effort. More than 170 countries and 4.9 million athletes participate in events including gymnastics, figure skating, track and field, and skiing. Over seventy thousand competitions are held every year. The World Games, like the Olympics and Paralympics, take place every two years, alternating between summer and winter.

CHAPTER 9
It Happened in Athens

The 2004 Games, held in Athens, were Tanni Grey-Thompson's fourth—and last—Paralympics. Going into the competition, the Welsh wheelchair racer had fourteen medals, nine of them gold. She was the first female athlete to break one minute in the 400m race.

Tanni Grey-Thompson

Already she was famous throughout the United Kingdom. Everyone would be watching her final four races.

Grey-Thompson felt excited about the first race, the 800m. It was always her strongest.

She came in seventh, her worst showing ever.

In the stands, friends and family cried. Grey-Thompson felt awful. But her two-year-old daughter didn't care who had won. "Can I have an ice cream?" she soon asked her mother. Immediately, Grey-Thompson felt better.

Still, she was very nervous for her second event. The 100m had always been her weakest race. Right before the start, she threw up. But a strange thing happened after she pushed off from the line. She saw one thing and one thing only: the finish line, straight ahead. Everything else— the crowd, the cheers—fell away. She was in the zone.

Grey-Thompson shot down the track. Halfway through the race, she pulled even with the lead racer. A few meters later, she edged past.

She won in 17.24 seconds, her personal best. She said that it was the most rewarding moment of her career.

In 2012, Tanni Grey-Thompson was honored off the track, too. Appointed to the British Parliament, she has been working in government to fight for people with disabilities.

There was also excitement in the indoor arena over wheelchair rugby. A game so fast and rough, it was originally called murderball.

Quadriplegic athletes, paralyzed in some way in all four limbs, use special wheelchairs. Players say their chairs become "gladiators," built to take a beating as racers crash into their opponents.

Playing on a basketball court in teams of four, rugby athletes hold a volleyball in their laps as they push their chairs but must bounce or pass the ball at least once every ten seconds.

Their mission: to get the ball across the goal line and score for their team.

In the semifinals in 2004, the United States was playing against Canada. The US team had won gold in 2000, but it had lost to Canada in the last World Championships. The teams were more than run-of-the-mill rivals, though. The Canadian coach had once been on the US team. So this game was personal.

It was a tight match. The teams stayed within a point of each other. Then in the final moments, Canada pulled ahead, point by point, winning 24–20. (Canada later lost to New Zealand in the finals.)

For the US players, it was an emotional finish and the toughest loss they could imagine. While the Canadians celebrated, they choked back tears, knowing they'd go home in third place.

Meanwhile, British athlete Lee Pearson was competing in a sport far different from rugby: equestrian dressage, an elegant horseback-riding event.

Pearson was born in 1974 with a rare disorder that affected his joints and muscles. He used crutches and had difficulty moving his arms. And although he continually fell off his first pony, his love of horses eventually led him to dressage.

In dressage routines, a rider and horse move

in pirouettes, zigzags, and half-turns, as well as in straight lines and sideways, at a walk, trot, and canter. The rider guides the horse with small movements, almost impossible to see. Yet the performance requires great effort and concentration—and for Pearson, a true connection with his horse.

Before Athens, Pearson had already won three gold medals in his first Paralympics. Could he repeat here? Yes! He did, even going on to three-peat in 2008.

But many remember Pearson more for one simple act of kindness in Athens. During one event, something unexpected and awful happened. A young French rider, Valerie Salles, entered the ring and almost immediately, her horse died. Pearson's heart went out to the teenager. Right after the medal ceremony, Pearson slid off his horse. Then he grabbed his crutches and presented Salles with his victory bouquet.

Lee Pearson and Valerie Salles

CHAPTER 10
Teammates and Rivals

At the Athens Games, American swimmer Erin Popovich won seven gold medals, one for each of her events. Born with a form of dwarfism, she put Paralympic swimming in the news.

Popovich's rival in the pool was another American, Jessica Long.

Erin Popovich   Jessica Long

After being adopted from a Russian orphanage as a baby, Long had to have both of her legs removed below the knee. She grew up in Baltimore, Maryland, determined to keep up with everyone else. In the water, she discovered she could be faster. Popovich was her idol.

In 2004, Long and Popovich swam together in a team relay race. They won gold. But they were competing against each other in Beijing, China. The event was the 100m breaststroke.

Sixteen-year-old Long had the world record, but Popovich held the Paralympic title. And it was Popovich who captured the gold again, setting a new world record: 1 minute, 31.60 seconds. "I never minded losing to her," Long later wrote in a book. But Long knew she could do better. In London at the 2012 Games, Long competed in the same race. Popovich was working at the Games, not swimming.

At the event, Long walked out to the pool deck,

looking confident. She took off her prosthetic legs and got ready to dive.

No one could catch her. She broke Popovich's world record with a 1 minute, 29.28 time, taking gold. But just like Lee Pearson, she decided to give away her bouquet. Long left the flowers, with a note, in Popovich's hotel room.

Erin Popovich was still her hero.

Swimmers Who Are Physically Disabled

Swimmers with a leg impairment enter the pool area wearing prosthetics or using a wheelchair. Assistants help them onto the diving platform or into the pool; no prosthetics are allowed while they're swimming. To start, athletes may stand

or sit on the diving platform, stand next to the platform, or float in the water. An athlete without arms competing in the backstroke can use a starting device—a strap, cord, or towel gripped between the teeth, while an assistant at the edge of the pool holds the other end. When the race begins, the swimmer releases the cord and pushes off.

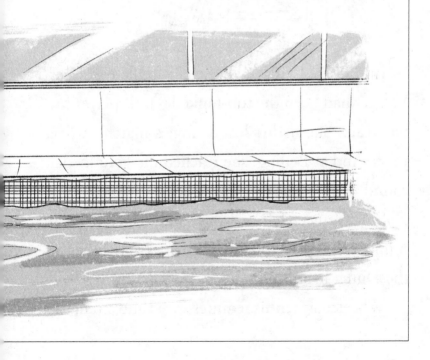

In 2008, Dutch wheelchair athlete Esther
Vergeer had been the top-ranked tennis player for
ten years. She hadn't lost a singles match in five
years. And at Beijing, she reached the gold medal
round without losing a single set.

Still, Vergeer felt nervous. She was facing the
number-two player, Korie Homan—a member of
the Dutch team, too.

Wheelchair tennis requires speed and strength.

Players have to move quickly, sometimes using one arm to steer their wheelchair while using their racquet arm to hit the ball hard. Vergeer won the first set. But at the end of the second set, she felt nervous again and was just "pushing the ball," she said later, hoping it would fall in a good spot. Homan was playing strong. She needed one more point to win.

Somehow, Vergeer found strength. She tied it

up. At that point, it was anybody's game. Homan served; Vergeer returned the ball easily. Could Homan get to it in time? Yes! Using her backhand, she sent the ball flying—right into the net.

Korie Homan at the 2008 Paralympic Games

Vergeer won the set, the match, and the gold.

She didn't stop there. Vergeer kept playing, right through the 2012 Paralympics, ending her career with seven gold medals and a 470-game winning streak.

CHAPTER 11
Unexpected Endings

The 2012 Summer Games were held in London. For the first time in twelve years, athletes with intellectual disabilities were back in the program.

Also, for the *very* first time, the small African nation of Rwanda sent a team to compete. Their sport? Sitting volleyball.

Sitting volleyball game

In sitting volleyball, players don't just sit. They throw their bodies around the small court. They smash the ball over the low net. Experts say the game is more challenging than the nondisabled version.

The Rwandan team didn't have experience or training. Their coach said that about all they had was a dream.

Well, that's not the whole story. In London, they had a very loyal following. People were rooting for them to win. Most of the players had limbs missing. Many had been injured during the country's civil war.

During the war, some players had fought for different sides. They had been enemies. But they'd put their pasts behind them. They were united, trying to represent their country the best way possible. "Actually," one player explained, "we are best friends."

So far at the Paralympics, they'd lost every

game. They had one last chance to win. In the final matchup, Rwanda versus Morocco, whoever was defeated would leave in last place. Neither team wanted that.

Rwanda lost the first set, 25–20.

But the second set hung in the balance. The volleys grew longer, the plays more intense. At one point, Rwanda was ahead, 18–14. Toward the end of the match, the teams swapped leads. When Morocco pulled ahead 22–20, Rwanda was more determined than ever.

The Rwandan Civil War, 1990–1993

Rwanda's civil war divided the small African country into two groups: Hutu, the vast majority, and Tutsi, the minority that had been in power until a government overthrow in 1959. After that, hundreds of thousands of Tutsis fled the country. Some formed a rebel organization that invaded Rwanda in 1990, starting a three-year conflict. One year later, in 1994 the Rwandan president, a Hutu, was killed. Hutus took revenge. Between five hundred thousand and one million people—primarily Tutsi—

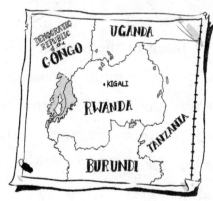

were killed. When it was over, a Hutu and a Tutsi leader headed up the new government.

Soon the score was 23–23, then 24–24, and then—because teams must win by two points—25–25.

Rwanda got the next point. Then they served. The Moroccan players thought the ball was going out of bounds. They didn't move.

The ball fell just inside the line. Rwanda won 27–25! With momentum on their side, they took the next two sets and the match.

Fans rose to their feet, cheering. Rwanda didn't come in last! For the players, it felt like a gold medal.

A surprise victory was in store for another fan favorite, too: American Matt Stutzman, the "Armless Archer." Born without arms, Stutzman grew up doing everything with his feet—from using a knife and fork to writing, playing guitar, and even shooting a bow and arrow.

Matt Stutzman

Stutzman wasn't expected to medal. He'd only taken up archery in his twenties. But he won silver in 2012. In 2015, he was ranked eleventh in the whole world of archery, nondisabled competitors included. And he broke his own record for longest accurate shot. While the Paralympic target is approximately 55 yards from the archer, his record-breaker was 310 yards away.

Despite having both legs amputated before he turned one, South Africa's Oscar Pistorius ran on prosthetics to break a world record at the 2004 Paralympics. But more than anything else, he wanted to compete in the Olympics.

Oscar Pistorius wins at the 2004 Paralympics

For a long time, that seemed impossible. A scientist determined that the prosthetic "blades" Pistorius used when competing gave him an unfair advantage. Finally he proved in court, with other scientists backing him, that it wasn't the case. And in 2012, he won a spot on South Africa's Olympic team.

Pistorius made it to the semifinals in the 400m and competed in the 400m relay. The team placed eighth. Still, Pistorius made history.

Next came the Paralympics. The biggest race there? The 100m. It featured Pistorius, the defending champion. Brazil's Alan Oliveira, who'd just beaten Pistorius in the 200m, was running, too, along with the 2008 silver medalist, American Jerome Singleton.

There was one more real contender: a little-known British runner, nineteen-year-old Jonnie Peacock. His first international race had been just four months earlier. Yet somehow, he held the world record.

"Peacock! Peacock!" London fans cheered for their fellow countryman. The starting gun sounded. The runners took off, neck and neck.

Para-Athletes at the Olympics

Oscar Pistorius is not the only athlete with a disability to compete in the Olympics. Way back in 1904, George Eyser represented the United States in gymnastics. Performing with a wooden leg, he won six medals. In the years to come, athletes with impairments have competed in table tennis, archery, and water polo. Denmark's Lis Hartel, paralyzed below the knees, became one of the first women to compete against men in any kind of equestrian event, winning silver. Other athletes include American runner Marla Runyan—who is legally blind and the first American to make appearances in the Olympics and Paralympics—finishing eighth in the 1500m in 2000; and South African swimmer Natalie du Toit, competing in the 2008 6.2 mile race through open water with an amputated leg.

Lis Hartel at the 1952 Olympic Games

About two-thirds of the way through, Peacock drew ahead. He crossed the finish line in 10.90 seconds, winning gold and setting a Paralympic record.

It was called one of the greatest moments in Paralympic history. None of the other front-runners even medaled—including Oscar Pistorius. But the competition wasn't over. Two days later, Pistorius took first place in the 400m. He ended the summer a winner and an international top runner. London, however, turned out to be his last Games.

Oscar Pistorius on Trial

Five months after the Paralympics, on Valentine's Day, 2013, the star athlete was arrested. He stood trial for the murder of his girlfriend, Reeva Steenkamp. Pistorius admitted to the shooting at his home in Pretoria, South Africa. His defense: He thought she was an intruder. But the court found him guilty. Eventually, Pistorius received a thirteen-year prison sentence. Now a fallen hero, his story rocked his country and the world of sports.

CHAPTER 12
All-Around Athletes

At the London Games, twenty-three-year-old American wheelchair racer Tatyana McFadden was already making her third appearance at the Paralympics. Born in Russia unable to move

below the waist, McFadden was adopted when she was six years old and brought to her new home in Maryland. She was so weak that doctors weren't sure how long she'd live. But sports saved her life, building her strength and determination.

Tatyana McFadden

In 2012, McFadden won

Tatyana (left) and Hannah McFadden, 2012

three gold medals in wheelchair racing. She also won a bronze in the 100m, while her little sister Hannah came in eighth. The two made history: the first siblings to ever make the US Paralympic Team.

American Oksana Masters made history, too. She and her partner were the first US pair to medal in their rowing event. This is a contest where an athlete needs a lot of strength in both the back and arms. Yet Masters had been born missing muscles in her arms.

Like McFadden, Masters was adopted from an Eastern European country—in her case, Ukraine—and became part of an American family. Besides having that in common, they were both heading to Sochi, Russia, to compete in the Winter Olympics—against each other. The event was sit skiing.

McFadden Goes to Court

Tatyana McFadden debuted in Athens in 2004, winning silver and bronze and knowing she'd found her passion. Just months later, she joined her high school track team. School officials said she could only race separately, alone on the track—not alongside her teammates. McFadden thought that was unfair. She and her family filed a lawsuit against the school system and won. The case paved the way for national laws guaranteeing that all students with disabilities have the equal right to participate in sports.

McFadden had never actually sit skied until the year before. Now in Sochi for the 2014 Winter Games, she was waiting at the starting line for the one-kilometer cross-country race to begin. (A kilometer is about two-thirds of a mile.)

The skiers pushed off in two groups. Those with a more severe impairment went first. At first they stayed in a pack. Together, they navigated the dips and rises in the course. Then the skiers began to separate. A few moved out in front. First Masters took the lead; then McFadden edged ahead.

Soon another skier gained ground. Mariann Marthinsen, from Sweden, closed in on McFadden. Just as she and McFadden approached the finish line, Marthinsen drew even. Then she inched ahead, the tip of her ski crossing the line first.

It was as close as it could get. First-time skier McFadden was thrilled with silver. She was just

as happy her entire family was there to watch. Masters came in fourth. But she left satisfied, too, taking home a silver and bronze.

Sochi would be McFadden's one and only Winter Games. But Masters came back for the next, in 2018 in PyeongChang, South Korea, better than ever, winning five medals: two gold, two silver, and a bronze.

Meanwhile, in 2016, they both went to Rio de Janeiro.

The 2016 Summer Paralympics in Brazil broke all TV viewing records: 4.1 billion people tuned in for the coverage in 154 countries.

At the Rio Games, McFadden was back to wheelchair racing. She won six medals, four of them gold.

Masters, meanwhile, took on a brand-new challenge: handcycling. The three-wheeled bikes are built low to the ground. They're powered by arms, not legs. Masters loved the speed.

She didn't medal. But that was all right. It was all about testing limits.

On the men's side of handcycling, Italian Alex Zanardi was back for his second Games.

For years, Zanardi had been a top-ranked race-car driver. In September 2001, he had the lead in a championship race. He pulled over for a pit stop. When he drove onto a side lane to get back on the track, he hit a wet patch. He spun out, right into the middle of the course.

Cars sped toward Zanardi at two hundred miles per hour. One slammed into him. Zanardi lost both legs, above the knee. But he felt lucky to be alive. And he found a new passion in handcycling.

In Rio, the twenty-kilometer race took place at the Olympic Stadium. It was built on an old race-car circuit. The course held special memories for Zanardi; he'd competed there as a driver. The date of the event, September 14, had meaning, too. His life-changing crash had happened almost exactly fifteen years earlier.

His old race course and the tragic anniversary—Zanardi took it all in stride. He won the gold.

Alex Zanardi

CHAPTER 13
2018 and Beyond

Next up in the Paralympic schedule were the 2018 Winter Games in PyeongChang, South Korea, featuring the crowd-pleasing sport of sled hockey.

Sled hockey is played like nondisabled ice hockey, but with two differences: Players use special sleds built on skate blades, and they hold a much smaller stick in each hand. One end has a razor-sharp pick—used for pushing the sled along the ice—while the other end is curved to hit the puck.

That year, the US sled hockey team was looking to set a record: three gold medals in a row. They knew it wouldn't be easy. For the first time at the Paralympics, the team faced Canada in the finals. The Canadians were the world champions and Team USA's biggest rivals.

Twelve minutes into the first period, Canada got a goal. The score stayed 1–0 through the first

period, the second, and even the third. With just over a minute left in the match, the US team had to do something big.

The coach pulled the goalie. He put an extra player on the ice, someone who could help the team score. But the net was left wide open.

Canada won the face-off, and forward Rob Armstrong sped away with the puck, a clear path ahead of him. It seemed like an easy Canadian goal. He shot—and hit the post.

There were seconds left on the clock. Team USA had the puck. They passed from player to player, moving down the ice. They crowded the net. A defenseman blocked a shot, and the puck bounced away.

American Declan Farmer trapped it. He fired the puck past the goalie, straight into the back of the net.

It was a tied game, right at the buzzer.

Three minutes into overtime, Farmer scored again. The United States won gold!

American downhill skier Danelle Umstead was at PyeongChang, too.

At thirteen years old, Danelle was diagnosed with a serious eye disease. Her vision got worse as she got older. It was her father who encouraged her to take up skiing. Danelle was in her late twenties by then. "What?" she replied. "We live in Texas [where there aren't any mountains].

And I'm blind!" Her dad promised to be there with her, every step of the way. And that was it; Danelle was hooked. In Vancouver in 2010, she competed with her husband as her guide.

In each race, Rob Umstead left the gate first. He wore colorful gear so Danelle could make out the bright colors and follow his path. They both wore headsets to communicate. And they won two bronze medals.

Danelle Umstead behind her guide and husband, Rob Umstead

Bad news came just after the victories. Danelle had multiple sclerosis, a disease that affects the brain, spinal cord, and nerves. After one attack, she had to learn to walk—and ski—all over again.

She still medaled at the 2014 Games. But could she compete at PyeongChang at age forty-six?

Yes, she decided. Danelle went into training, knowing she'd have bad days. But she didn't want anything to stop her—not her vision, not her age, and not the new health problem.

Nothing was going to stop Amy Purdy, either.

Amy Purdy

Growing up in Las Vegas, Purdy always wanted to be a pro snowboarder. But when she was nineteen years old, an infection almost took her life. She lost both legs below the knee.

Purdy had never missed a snowboard season before.

And she intended to keep on going. She taught herself to snowboard with prosthetics. It was a struggle. Her knees didn't bend and her ankles couldn't flex. Bit by bit, she learned. And she became the first female in the world to snowboard competitively with two prosthetics.

After that, Purdy wanted to compete in the Paralympics. However, there was just one problem: Snowboarding wasn't an event.

Purdy pushed and pushed to get her sport on the program. And in 2014, it was—with groundbreaking snowboarder Amy Purdy winning bronze.

In the lead-up to the 2018 Games, Purdy developed muscle disorders in her arms. She stopped competing. She stopped training. But then slowly she worked her way back into shape. At PyeongChang, she medaled twice. It had been a tough but worthwhile battle. "I'm ready to keep this going," she said just after the Paralympics.

So? Which other Paralympians are thinking of returning?

British cyclist Sarah Storey was born without a functioning left hand. At Rio de Janeiro she became Great Britain's most decorated female athlete. In 2020, at the Tokyo Games, she's planning to race in four events. Will she unseat Mike Kenny for the country's number-one spot?

American David Brown became the fastest totally blind runner in the world—the first to finish the 100m in under eleven seconds. With his guide, Jerome Avery, he won gold in Rio. He's sure to be back.

What about Egyptian table tennis star Ibrahim Hamadtou? He became a YouTube sensation and was the only athlete without arms to compete in the sport. Holding the paddle in his mouth and tossing the ball with his bare foot, he plays like a pro.

Tatyana McFadden is the only wheelchair racer to win four straight marathon Grand Slams—earning first place in the biggest marathons in the world. But in the Paralympic event, she's only won silver. Will she make it to Tokyo and add a title there?

These athletes break records; they reach new heights. And sometimes, they best Olympians.

In the Rio Paralympics, Algeria's Abdellatif Baka, a visually impaired runner, won gold in the 1500m race. The next three runners were close behind. How fast was the race? All four beat the

gold medal time for the same Olympic event held just weeks earlier.

The Paralympic Games have grown from a handful of competitors trying to improve their health to thousands of elite athletes focused on one thing: competition.

These athletes believe anything is possible. And at the Paralympics, they prove it.

Timeline of the Paralympic Games

1948 — First Stoke Mandeville Games for the Paralyzed are held on July 29 for patients with spinal cord injuries

1952 — The Games become international when a team from the Netherlands competes at Stoke Mandeville

1960 — Considered the first international Paralympics, the Games take place in Rome, the same site as the Olympics

1976 — The first Winter Games are held in Sweden

— The Summer Games add other disability groups

1980 — Summer Games record-holder Trischa Zorn, with fifty-five medals, competes at her first Paralympics

1988 — The Games are officially named the Paralympics

1994 — German skier Reinhild Möller receives a $1 million contract, paving the way for more Paralympian funding

2000 — Spain's basketball team for athletes with intellectual disabilities is disqualified for including semipro players without impairment

2004 — Canadian racer Chantal Petitclerc turns down a shared Athlete of the Year award as a protest for all athletes with disabilities

2012 — South African sprinter Oscar Pistorius becomes the first double leg amputee to compete in the Olympics

2018 — The US sled hockey team wins its record third gold medal

Timeline of the World

1948 — Known for his nonviolent protests, Mahatma Gandhi, leader of India's independence movement, is assassinated on January 30

1952 — New York City installs its first "Don't Walk" stop sign

1955 — The first polio vaccine is administered throughout the United States

1960 — John F. Kennedy and Richard Nixon face off in the first televised presidential debate

1976 — On April 1, Apple Computer is founded by Steve Jobs and Steve Wozniak

1980 — Washington State's volcano, Mount St. Helens, erupts on May 18, killing fifty-seven people

1988 — NASA scientist James Hansen testifies in US Congress, warning US lawmakers about climate change

1994 — The World Series is canceled due to a Major League Baseball players' strike

2000 — Venus Williams wins her first women's singles title at Wimbledon tennis championships

2003 — China becomes the third country to send an astronaut into space

2012 — In January, the luxury cruise ship *Costa Concordia* hits the rocky Italian shoreline and capsizes on Friday the thirteenth

Bibliography

*Books for young readers

Britain, Ian. *From Stoke Mandeville to Sochi: A History of the Summer and Winter Paralympic Games.* Champagne, IL: Common Ground Publishing, 2012.

Goodman, Susan. *Spirit of Stoke Mandeville: The Story of Sir Ludwig Guttmann.* London: Collins Publishers, 1986.

*Long, Jessica, with Hannah Long. *Unsinkable: From Russian Orphanage to Paralympic Swimming World Champion.* New York: Houghton Mifflin Harcourt, 2018.

*McFadden, Tatyana, and Tom Walker. *Tatyana McFadden: Ya Sama! Moments from My Life.* N.p.: InspiredEdge Editions, 2016.

Wood, Cathy. *The True Story of Great Britain's Paralympic Heroes.* London: Carlton Books Limited, 2011.

Website

https://www.paralympic.org

A javelin event at the Stoke Mandeville Games, 1955

An archery competition at the Stoke Mandeville Games, 1955

Dr. Ludwig Guttmann

Team Japan at the opening ceremony of the
International Stoke Mandeville Games in Tokyo, 1964

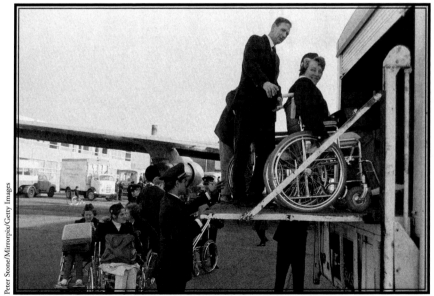

The British team leaving for the
International Stoke Mandeville Games in Israel, 1968

Mike Kenny with his swimming medals from the
Seoul 1988 Paralympic Games

Louise Sauvage celebrates her win at the Sydney 2000 Paralympic Games.

Henry Wanyoike (right) setting a new world record during
the Athens 2004 Paralympic Games

A sled hockey match at the Sochi 2014 Paralympic Games

Erin Popovich in the women's 100m freestyle at
the Beijing 2008 Paralympic Games

Matt Stutzman competes in archery at the London 2012 Paralympic Games.

Alex Zanardi celebrates winning the men's individual road race at
the London 2012 Paralympic Games.

Jessica Long in the women's 400m freestyle final at
the Rio 2016 Paralympic Games

Tatyana McFadden leads the women's 5000m final at
the Rio 2016 Paralympic Games.

Ibrahim Hamadtou competes in table tennis at
the Rio 2016 Paralympic Games.

Jonnie Peacock leads the men's 100m final at
the Rio 2016 Paralympic Games.

Oksana Masters wins a women's cross-country skiing final at
the PyeongChang 2018 Paralympic Games.

Danelle Umstead and her guide Rob Umstead (with mouthpiece) at the PyeongChang 2018 Paralympic Games

Marcia Malsar holding the Paralympic torch during the opening ceremony of the Rio 2016 Paralympic Games